HOSPITAL ISSUED WRITING NOTEBOOK

Hospital Issued Writing Notebook

Dan Flore III

QUERENCIA

Querencia Press, LLC
Chicago, Illinois

QUERENCIA PRESS

© Copyright 2023
Dan Flore III

LIBRARY OF CONGRESS CATALOGING-IN-PUBLICATION DATA

ISBN 978 1 959118 17 6

www.querenciapress.com

First Published in 2023

Querencia Press, LLC
Chicago IL

Printed & Bound in the United States of America

*I think of everything I create as a miracle because
I did it in spite of my disability.*

C O N T E N T S

i'm not well and i want it to end
i'm out of my gabapentin pills which ease
both bi-polar and acute anxiety
i lay on the couch
like a corpse
taking heavy breaths
my apartment is a whirlpool
where i muster enough energy
to wade through it,
go out and smoke some holy balm toblacko
and pray "Jesus, Jesus, Jesus..."
desperate and at His big toe
which twitches with compassion
i can't see this though
unlike nights before
where eerily i would say to myself
someone else is here
and see His mystical feet
no now i'm in the wilderness of my brain
my wife asks if i need anything
and i say a lobotomy
cracked windshield eyes
and once one disease starts
the rest say hey we can have our way with him too
so on comes the sinus infection and psychotic thoughts
PTSD flashbacks
i text a friend who understands
her return messages

roll in like unfolding flowers
the kind you would bring to someone in the hospital

i can't eat
nerves shot
there are bullets in my belly
i'm weak with no sustenance
i complain and make noises
like a car that won't turn over
check engine light blinking in my chest
the pills i need don't work but they help
and help is what i need
i do ten deep breaths like they taught me in the mental
hospital
that offers some relief for about 10 seconds
i'm a piece of driftwood
all worn away and still getting wrecked
wrinkles in my face like the lines in that lumber
lost in the whirlpool sea
waiting for that pharmacy refill
living the nothingness
dying to something
i like whispers
whisper for me
a whisper is so gentle and sad
like a tissue
i could use for the tears
i should be crying

I wish an oak tree leaf would fall on me
I could use the caress

or I' d like to watch
a cigarette burn in an ashtray—
the devastation turning to ashes

my bee stung mind
longs for these things

but there' s only my boring phone
and my lung tornado of panic

isn' t there a wish for me
like a candle on a birthday cake?

I would blow and blow
at it
as a breathing exercise
till I calmed down
and wished for a never-ending purr

give me a passing glance
just a little recognition of me
a brief smile
before turning down the block

I would paint that smile in honey
on my sketchbook
and let the page get caught up in the wind
and fly

I am captive to the shudder
my only escape is in a giggle fit

get me outta here
take me where
the ripples are a lake laughing
I wanna swim the hysterics

Anything new is good. Even something
as mundane as gaining the privilege
to do your own laundry. I'm so
bored doing the laundry is actually
fun.

STANDING OVER MYSELF,
YELLING AT ME

lying down
with myself standing over me
yelling and trying to help
What do you need?!!
A cigarette?!!
A pill?!!
Your book?!!
WHAT WILL MAKE YOU FEEL BETTER?!!
I don't know what to do to help you!
I just wanna lie here, I respond
THAT'S NOT GONNA HELP!!
It will
when you shut up

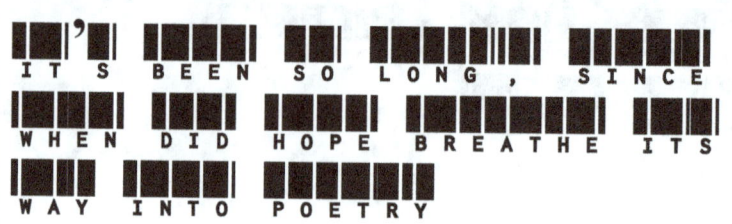

IT'S BEEN SO LONG, SINCE WHEN DID HOPE BREATHE ITS WAY INTO POETRY

Since when did the doves descend in the stanzas? I saw
one I think. She was like a mother to me, holding me in
her ruffles. I wanted to stay. The dirt under my
fingernails has been used for ink for so long I forgot
these verses could keep me in Christ's hair, bobbing in
a skyway of deliverance. Since when does hope exist at
all? I've been breathing the fumes with the garage door
down. I could use the air. Death is only following this
simple plan with the towels blocking the bottom to keep
the carbon monoxide in. Believe me, I know that's the
way my grandfather went and I keep circling the stupid
cottage where he did it. This is an appeal to sympathy
as I'm chained to his eyes, the way he smoked a
cigarette, even his brand. O Grampy, forgive me for not
honoring your misery, amen. Days without any human
contact in Cape May. How miserable was the sunlight?
You didn't even leave a note to explain. Send a dove
through my verses I need to breathe from the white flap
under her wings, there's nothing here but a panic
attack of your memory.

IMAGING ADVICE FROM MY OLD PSYCHIATRIST

I wish I could talk to my old psychiatrist
not as an official appointment
but just to get together
I imagine myself saying to him
it feels like my intestines are in a blender—
I have no peace
then I picture him replying,
Dan, what I want you to do
is go out to breakfast with your wife
order the wheat toast
and imagine
a long wheat field swaying in the breeze
and he would write out a real prescription
for me
for wheat toast

Everybody here wants to hook up w/ each other

a psychotic break is twisting your ankle and wanting
to. rockets being shit on by birds. the whole world
could look ugly or beautiful or both at the same time.
i had one in 1999 when they were delivering a playhouse
that looked like a demented alice in wonderland. i only
remember laying in a field, and the grass in my head
and on the ground, and walking in mud even though there
wasn't any. cops seem like authority figures from hell
when they come to get you, and all you see is blue, a
raging blue, ready to kick your ass. a psychotic break
is seeing nothing but the small breasts of the nurse
who treats you and the allergic reaction to the meds
and her eyes. it's a wide-angle lens that's too wide
and shattered. you feel like you're floating, with
guns in your brain that you don't want to go off
through your hands. it's the devil kissing you, sweet
as chocolate drizzle that comes down on you like
bolts lightning. you can't stop, you keep walking.
everyone can see you're deranged and the shame
intensifies your delusion which is a mirage of another
world. the ambulance siren in the dark is the dark. you
wanna jump out of it and tumble along the highway.
there's a demon orgy inside your stomach and your
perverted eyes keep peeking in. your sanity is in the
way your psychotic break drifts through the air and you
try to catch it and get out the door before they come
for you. a psychotic break is peeling the forbidden
banana but there's no fruit inside. You wanna grab
beauty and make it ugly but you don't, your last fleck

of sanity prevents you. you' re a danger to
yourself and others and the psychiatrist asks if
you are and you lie trying to stay out of the
hospital which will only make you more crazy. all
that' s left years later are the flashbacks. home
movies that let you live in them all over again.
you step carefully into your psychosis not meaning
to, but there' s nothing else on tv.

If somebody flips out they put
that person in "the quiet room"
This room is never quiet.

had a small panic attack
outside of the pharmacy

I was sitting out on the curb
in the blah white of February
with pieces of salt cracking
too loud under my sneaker

I had just been in the store and
they had boxes and shit
taking up the aisles

it was crowded too
so everyone was bumping
into each other

I had no money
so I was just aimlessly
drifting around in there
with no real purpose
other than

trying to
avoid my dad
who was ashamed to be
buying adult diapers
and was trying to hide it
from me

and I went along with it
like I didn't know

it was taking a long time
in the store
and I was staring at a pair of scissors
when I heard my dad
having an argument
with the manager
over a pack of Depends

that's when I went out for a cigarette
with this old lady staring at me
as I wandered again idly
in the parking lot
until I stopped on the curb
paranoid of getting smoke
near someone
then paranoid even more
of a cop pulling in
wondering what I was up to

that's when it got me
three little shots
of not being able to breathe
nobody knew it happened
and it was over pretty fast

I started to worry
if my dad had suffered too
he had been getting so stressed
at the manager
I wondered if he may have wet himself

when I finally met him
at the car he was complaining
about how he didn't know where I was
and I knew the whole trip
wasn't worth it

I hate cheese popcorn. They gave that out
for snack time today. I ate it and it
was delicious.

I'm scared
to meet
the pizza delivery guy
at the door
that's what happens
when you have social anxiety
maybe I won't have to meet him
if it keeps going like this
I can cancel my order
because I'm so nervous
I can't eat

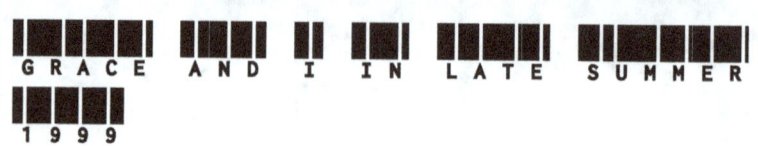

GRACE AND I IN LATE SUMMER

1999

Grace was a nursery rhyme
a lullaby in the daytime

she was there
after I
got out of the hospital
from my first
nervous breakdown

naps with her
in the afternoon
when I was so tired
and I got so tired
we were in my parents' bed
with the dresser and the bed stands
snoozing with us
the green outside the window
so quiet

we sat at picnic tables
and I'd read to her
about pretty demons
that were seducing me
even more than she was

she rocked me like a baby
with her words

24

the summer swaying
back & forth above us
just like a hammock
with a good book

I had a habit of self-punishment
and I'd burn myself with cigarettes
she'd see me sometimes and say
"Dan, what are you doing?"
like a mother figure
and I'd pull the cigarette away from my skin
like a child who just got caught

her long, pillow blonde hair
that I would rest my head on
her ocean lull blue eyes

she was the only one
my parents would allow to be with me
when they weren't around
we could trust Grace
her tiny hand in mine

bird singing gentleness
she could tuck me away
in the tuft below her wings

she's been gone for a very long time
but her figure still stands over me
her hand is still on my forehead
nurturing me in my sickness
through the sweetness of her memory

HALLUCINATING WHILE MY FRIEND SMOKES POT AND LOOKS AT ME LIKE I'M JESUS

I see things that aren't there
my friend thinks it's cool
says I'm a poet having visions

but I'm sick and they're hallucinations
so I wish he would shut the hell up about how awesome
it is
but he doesn't, he just goes on and on—

"you're like Ginsberg and Yeats...visions man!"
"ya gotta heal the tribe!"
"come on Lizard King, what visions are you seeing?"

I'm sick, you jerk! I say
and I ask him to leave
but I don't get him out
God, it's hard to get a hallucination to go away

It's very weird to have somebody watch you shave. Especially when you know they're there to make sure you don't try to kill yourself.

I will eventually get relief from this anxiety. I will. Scribble, scribble. Inhale on the end of a cigarette. I am ok in the spaces. The spaces where no one exists. My poison caterpillar eyebrows are crawling across my face. Weird light and smoke that isn't there. Jesus hanging out on the guardrail. A big truck. 5 seconds of calm wondering where he is hauling his load and how long he's been on the road. Then an engine rev from a sports car like a caveman beating his wife. My brain itches. The calm is gone. The sound of my phone is the unloading of 5 rounds. The mail is stress delivered to my heartbeat. Pound, pound, like a boxing glove. Rush hour breathing. The tick of the second hand is a sermon. But that too shall pass. The crash of people dumping garbage trashes me. Flowers on the table. Yes, I'll look at the flowers on the table to calm down. Somebody's screaming. It's me. Tears are God's balm. I can't eat but I'm starving. Force down a piece of bread (no butter.) I remember the bushes, holy in the moonlight and dark telling me, remember when you could talk yourself to peace and how that's gone now? Lost in my room in my childhood home. Grabbing my forehead of worry. Hell flashing in my face. Clutch the hand of God. I am exploding. 10 deep breaths. I have to leave. I can't go anywhere. Bed bugs eating sleep. If only a holy oil would pour all over. Doom is my constant companion. My stomach is filled with termites. Everything shuts the hell up...my meds just kicked in...

the supermarket
is swarming me
like a swat team
I only wanted a banana

a cool gray sky like ashes

I sit underneath it

unknown

psychotic

I search out the Nazarene
I bandage my eyes
it hurts just to look

smoking two cigarettes in a row

I have a cup of thirst

I'm afraid of myself

thoughts like cannon balls
exploding my skeleton

I am a dead young boy
I am a sick man
I wear my illness like a mugshot
but I am innocent as a snow cone

I drip slowly
I' m as tired as the summer that passed

bring me your pitiful pennies
make wishes in the fountain for me with them
I will pay you back with my thumb roses

alone, destitute

but I' m closer to god than I' ve ever been
knowing that I' m so far away from paradise

Smoking is prohibited. If you wanna make friends
join in the bitching about how stupid a rule it
is and how much you want a cigarette.

PILLBOXED

I'm
on
so
many
medications
for
mental
illness
it's
making
me
crazy

THERE'S A WHOLE WORLD OF SOCIAL ANXIETY JUST WAITING FOR YOU OUT THERE!

honk of a horn, then a retaliatory honk back. Maniacal
children waiting to swallow your face like a Lego.
glares of people for smoking, even though you're 12
feet away from them. broken pieces of cement scraping
together in your lungs. a robot that doesn't want you
to insert or swipe but to put in your pin(head.)
pedestrians have the wrong away. her cart takes up the
whole aisle. he's going in the ladies' room. they're
teenage thugs that came out to laugh at everybody.
we're out of money. i caught my breath with a bear
trap, now i can't get it out of it. you are doing
twice the speed limit. a carousel of insanity is
rolling down the street and its riders are eating
popcorn. get off the road! no turn on dead. head lice
rice. the juicy fart of paranoia. don't stand by my
car. the check engine light is winking at you from the
bar. dehydrated, recycled sunlight falling to the
ground like a nuclear meltdown and a one-dollar fee for
cash back. give a penny. take a penny. give a shit.
take a shit. give me a receipt for no reason other than
to have something to throw away. call an ambulance.
strap me to the siren blare all the way to the hospital
so they can give me pills that don' t work for all of
this.

I got my cigarettes and water
I' m sitting on the deck
I can' t hang with reality
I' m in another place
everything is going slow
slow as the fake flowers
sitting in a decorative bucket
I like how green they are
they almost look alive
and so do I
the noise of the cars is really bothersome
but birds start flying above me
and I am lost in their flight, it feels good
I don' t wonder about much
I haven' t got the strength for a daydream
I' m waiting for the sickness to pass
my mind should be coming around soon
I' ll talk to you when it does
until then let me sip my water and smoke my cigarettes
and don' t think I don' t see you look out on the deck
with sympathy
at this phantom of smoke who has taken my place

he had to fit me in

and she was so taken aback

by the great Dr. Quack's generosity to do that

and so was he

that they never bothered to ask

if the date they scheduled

was ok with me

Discharge today: realizing while
exchanging phone numbers with the
people I've grown close to that
we will never call each other.

desperately trying
to get my psych meds refilled
the woman on the phone
couldn't do much
but say goodbye, Dan
and I wonder if it is

this woman on the radio
was just talking about the glory of God
she said heaven opened up and she could hear music
playing

today the sink smells like puke
and the lighting is worse
I'm not doing anything about it either
and I'm too sick and broke to get outta here

why can't I reach into heaven too and hear just one
note playing for me
I need it on this godforsaken day
that I am only made of tears

last night I drank something that tasted
like an old lady's perfume
I've been puking and crapping and crying ever since

I like to think what I drank was the old lady's perfume
who was talking about heaven
and all these sounds my body has been making
are the music of heaven I'm hearing
that I've been wanting to hear so bad

heaven crying my body out with theirs
on their knees next to me by the toilet

I FELT SO SECURE I EVEN WANTED THE FLIES THERE

I was sick

reading the bible given to me by a friend

I kept thinking

I was going into the blessing he put on it

and back into his childhood bible lessons as I read the
verses

but when I got to Noah's ark

I thought of everybody in our apartment

my wife, me, our cat, and even the flies

on an ark

floating on my madness

and safe from it

all tucked in the bed sheets together